To my little sweetheart
on his first day at School
– TUESDAY, 10 SEPTEMBER 1991 –

All my love,
　　　　　Auntie Freed
　　　　　　xxxx

my first picture dictionary

Anne Civardi

Illustrated by
Graham Philpot

Consultant: Betty Root

Conran Octopus

All about this dictionary

This colourful, highly amusing picture dictionary will be enjoyed by all young children. The very young will love to share it with an adult, turning over the pages and talking about the delightful and lively pictures. They will have great fun discovering The Word Gang – Ollie Octopus, Millie Mouse, Patsy Pig, Boris Bear and all their friends – who appear throughout the book getting up to all sorts of antics while helping to illustrate the meaning of the words.

Those children who have just started to read will not find the text difficult because great care has been taken to ensure that the pictures give the right clues to the sentences underneath. The sentences put the words into context and in association with the pictures convey their meaning.

As it is a first word book, only nouns and verbs have been used. The nouns are in **grey** print and the verbs in **blue**. It will be helpful to explain to children that words which are the names of people and things are called nouns. Words that tell you what the animals are doing are called verbs.

Because this is a dictionary, the words are in alphabetical order. By using this book frequently, children will begin to learn where letters occur in the alphabet. This is a very important skill which will help them in many ways.

My First Picture Dictionary has outstanding and very original illustrations, and because of the humour, the colour and the content, children will want to return to it again and again. Through the joy of using it they will learn lots of new words and how to read and spell them.

Betty Root

Reading and Language Consultant
University of Reading

Noun
kangaroo

Kelly is a **kangaroo**.

Verb
blowing

Millie Mouse is **blowing** out the candle.

The Word Gang

Ellie Elephant
Millie Mouse
Gertie Giraffe
Sam Squirrel
Molly Monkey and baby
Freddie Frog
Bill Bird
Old Croc
Kelly Kangaroo and me
Boris Bear
Hilda Hippo
Patsy Pig
Leo Lion
Ollie Octopus
Roger Rabbit
Dudley Dog
Willie Worm
Derek Duck
Carly Cat

This is The Word Gang. Look for these animals in the book and find out what each of them gets up to.

abcdefghijklmnopqrstuvwxyz

Aa

alphabet
The first letter of the **alphabet** is a.

animals
Four furry **animals** standing in a row.

aeroplane
Derek Duck is flying the **aeroplane**.

ambulance
The **ambulance** is going to the hospital.

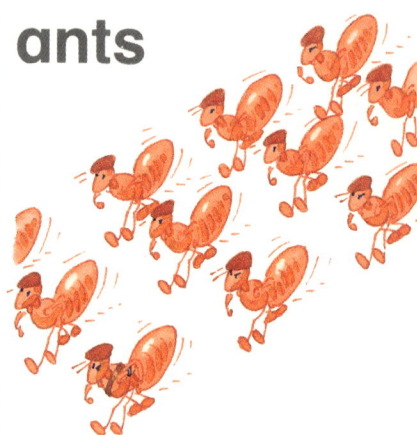

ants
Marching red **ants**.

airport
Derek Duck is landing at the **airport**.

angel
The **angel** is singing.

apple
Willie Worm is eating a green **apple**.

abcdefghijklmnopqrstuvwxyz

apron

Patsy Pig is wearing a frilly **apron**.

Bb

bag

The brown **bag** is full of money.

arrow

The **arrow** has hit the tree trunk.

baby

The **baby** is playing.

baker

The **baker** has baked a loaf of bread.

astronaut

Boris, the **astronaut**, is floating in space.

badges

Gertie Giraffe has six coloured **badges**.

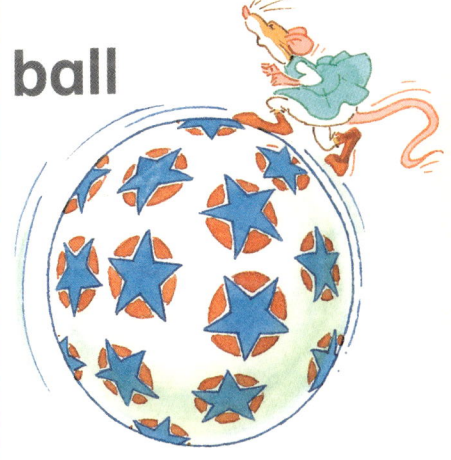

ball

Millie Mouse is walking on the **ball**.

5

a**b**cdefghijklmnopqrstuvwxyz

balloon

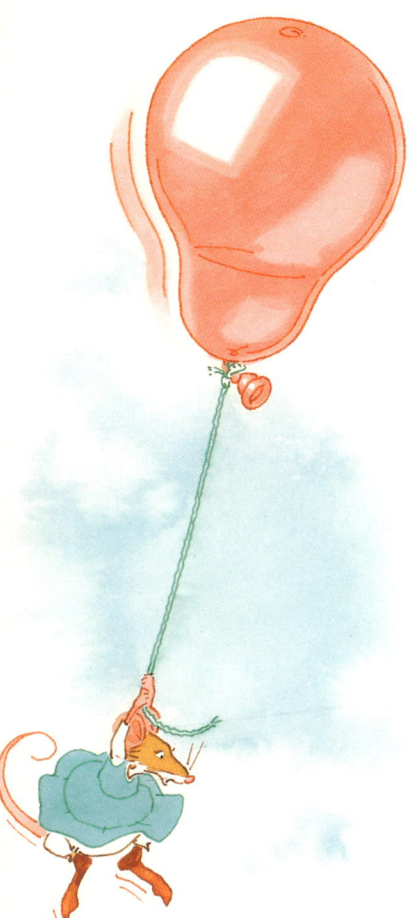

Millie Mouse is hanging on to the **balloon**.

band

The animals are playing in the **band**.

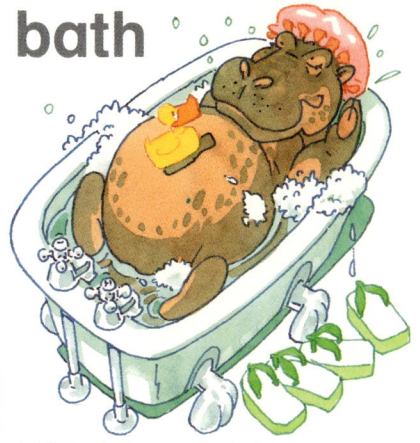

bath

Hilda Hippo is lying in the **bath**.

basket

The **basket** is full of smelly fish.

beans

A plate of **beans**.

bananas

A big bunch of ripe, yellow **bananas**.

bat

Roger Rabbit has a baseball **bat**.

bear

Boris is a happy **bear**.

a**b**cdefghijklmnopqrstuvwxyz

bed
Gertie Giraffe has a very long **bed**.

belt
Boris Bear's red and yellow **belt**.

blowing
Millie Mouse is **blowing** out the candle.

bee
The **bee** gets honey from the flower.

bicycle
Molly Monkey is riding her **bicycle**.

boat
Ollie Octopus is rowing the **boat**.

bell
Millie Mouse is ringing the **bell**.

bird
Bill is a big **bird**.

bone
Dudley Dog has a big, juicy **bone**.

7

a b c d e f g h i j k l m n o p q r s t u v w x y z

book
Willie Worm is busy reading his **book**.

bottom
Molly Monkey is at the **bottom** of the slide.

boy
Jake is a **boy**.

boot
A big, brown **boot**.

bowl
A **bowl** of hot porridge for Boris Bear.

branch
Two little birds on a big **branch**.

bottle
A **bottle** of fizzy beer.

box
Carly Cat is asleep in the **box**.

bread
Millie is nibbling a hole in the loaf of **bread**.

a b c d e f g h i j k l m n o p q r s t u v w x y z

breakfast
Two eggs and toast for **breakfast**.

brushing
Leo Lion is **brushing** his long mane.

building
Bill Bird is **building** a big nest.

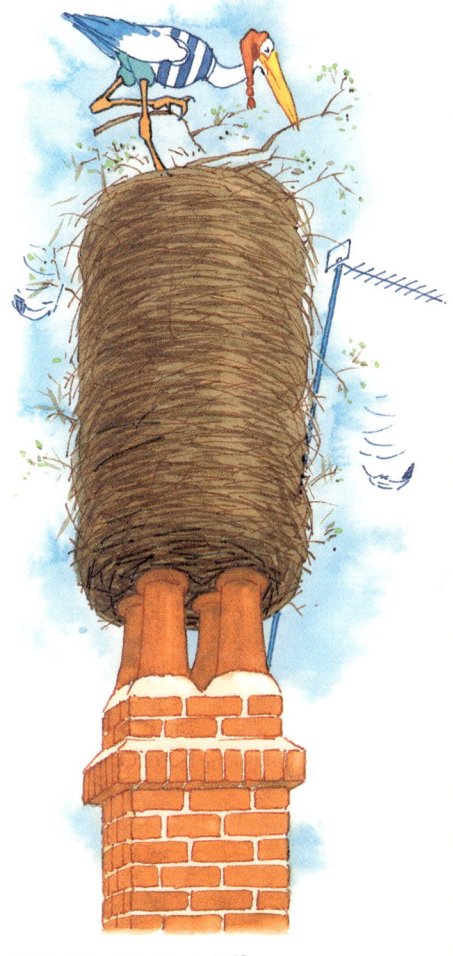

brick
Roger Rabbit is carrying a heavy **brick**.

bubble
Molly Monkey is blowing a big, round **bubble**.

bridge
The boat is going under the **bridge**.

bucket
Freddie Frog peeps out of the **bucket**.

bull
An angry **bull**.

a b c d e f g h i j k l m n o p q r s t u v w x y z

bulldozer

Derek Duck is driving a yellow **bulldozer**.

butcher

The **butcher** is chopping up meat.

Cc

bus

The **bus** stops at the bus stop.

butter

Millie Mouse is smelling the **butter**.

cabbage

The tortoise likes eating lots of **cabbage**.

bush

A bird in a **bush**.

butterfly

A big, beautiful, blue **butterfly**.

cage

The tiger prowls around the **cage**.

10

a b **c** d e f g h i j k l m n o p q r s t u v w x y z

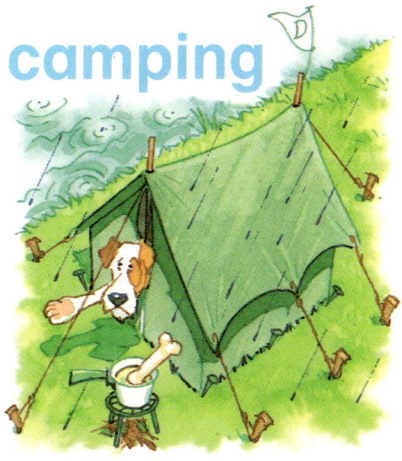

cake
A big, chocolate **cake**.

camping
Dudley Dog is **camping** in the rain.

car
Derek Duck has a shiny yellow sports **car**.

camel
Derek Duck is riding a **camel**.

candle
There is one **candle** on the cake.

carpet
Carly Cat rolls out the **carpet**.

camera
Boris Bear takes pictures with his **camera**.

cap
Roger Rabbit is wearing a red **cap**.

carrot
Roger Rabbit munches on the big **carrot**.

a**b**c**d**e**f**g**h**i**j**k**l**m**n**o**p**q**r**s**t**u**v**w**x**y**z**

castle

There is a moat around the **castle**.

catching

Roger Rabbit is **catching** the ball.

caterpillar

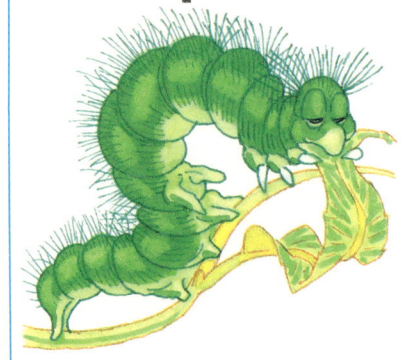

A big, green, hairy **caterpillar**.

cave

A dark, spooky **cave**.

chair

Freddie Frog sits on the **chair**.

cat

Carly is a sleepy **cat**.

cauliflower

Ellie Elephant has picked a **cauliflower**.

chasing

Carly Cat is **chasing** the mouse.

abcdefghijklmnopqrstuvwxyz

cheese
Millie Mouse loves eating **cheese**.

chicken
The **chicken** has laid a big, brown egg.

chocolate
Old Croc is eating a bar of **chocolate**.

cherries
The ripe **cherries** are on the branch.

children
The **children** are playing.

Christmas
Ollie Octopus gets lots of presents at **Christmas**.

chess
Willie and Millie are playing **chess**.

chimney
Santa Claus goes down the **chimney**.

church
The **church** is on top of the hill.

13

ab**c**defghijklmnopqrstuvwxyz

circle
The ducks swim in a big **circle**.

clock
The cuckoo comes out of the **clock**.

coat
Boris Bear has a smart blue **coat**.

cleaning
Patsy Pig is **cleaning** the mirror.

cloud
Bill Bird flies through the **cloud**.

combing
Leo Lion is **combing** his long whiskers.

climbing
Molly Monkey is **climbing** up the rope.

clown
The **clown** is making a funny face.

comic
The **comic** is full of funny pictures.

abcdefghijklmnopqrstuvwxyz

computer

Molly Monkey is working on her **computer**.

cow

The brown **cow** has a little calf.

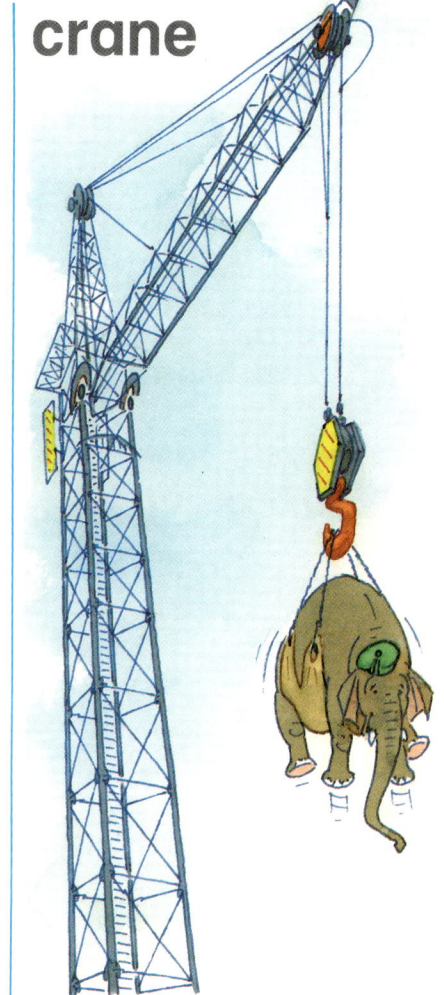

crane

The **crane** lifts up Ellie Elephant.

cooking

Patsy Pig is **cooking** dinner for Boris.

cowboy

Roger is pretending to be a **cowboy**.

counting

Boris Bear is **counting** his money.

crab

The **crab** is walking across the sand.

crashing

The cars are **crashing** into each other.

abcdefghijklmnopqrstuvwxyz

crayon
Millie Mouse is drawing with a red **crayon**.

crown
The king is wearing a golden **crown**.

cup
This is Boris Bear's best **cup**.

crocodile
Old Croc is a very old **crocodile**.

crying
Old Croc is **crying**.

curtain
Bill Bird is behind the **curtain**.

crossing
Kelly Kangaroo is **crossing** the road.

cucumber
Roger Rabbit is slicing the **cucumber**.

cutting
Molly Monkey is busy **cutting** the hedge.

abc**d**efghijklmnopqrstuvwxyz

Dd

dancing
Patsy Pig loves **dancing** with Boris Bear. 

deer
The **deer** has spiky antlers on his head.

daffodils
A beautiful bunch of yellow **daffodils**.

dark
It is **dark** outside.

dentist
The **dentist** is mending Molly Monkey's teeth.

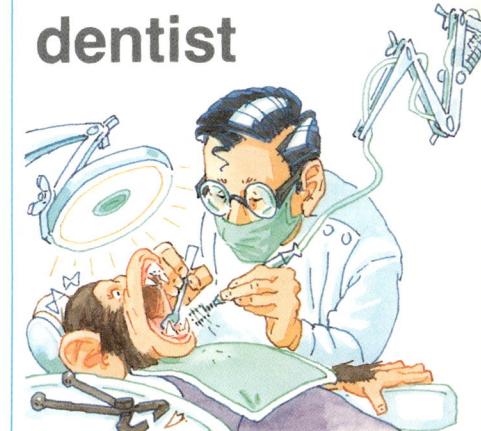

dancer
Patsy Pig wants to be a famous **dancer**.

deep
Freddie Frog is swimming in **deep** water.

desert
It is very hot and dry in the **desert**.

abc**d**efghijklmnopqrstuvwxyz

desk
Willie Worm is working at his **desk**.

diving
Freddie Frog is **diving** off a high rock.

dog
Dudley is a dirty **dog**.

digging
Dudley Dog is **digging** a deep hole.

doll
The **doll** has lots of curly red hair.

dinosaur
A big, green **dinosaur**.

doctor
The **doctor** listens to Hilda Hippo's heart.

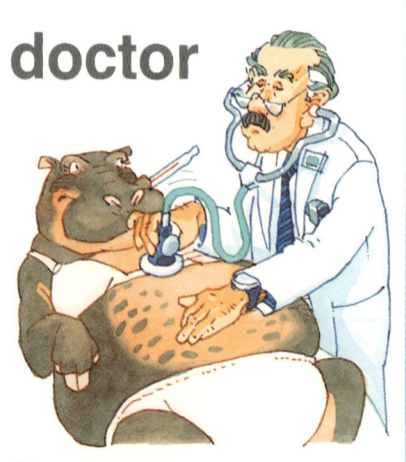

dolphin
The **dolphin** is jumping out of the water.

18

abc**d**efghijklmnopqrstuvwxyz

donkey

Roger Rabbit is riding on a **donkey**.

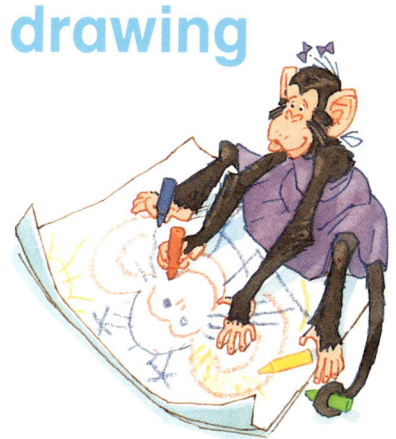

drawing

Molly Monkey is **drawing** a picture of herself.

driving

Derek Duck is **driving** his new sports car.

door

Ellie Elephant opens the **door** with her trunk.

dress

Patsy Pig is wearing her favourite **dress**.

drum

Boris Bear beats the big **drum**.

dragon

The **dragon** has wings and breathes fire.

drinking

Molly Monkey is **drinking** a glass of orange juice.

duck

Derek is a busy **duck**.

abcd**e**fghijklmnopqrstuvwxyz

Ee

eating

Boris Bear is **eating** his lunch.

envelope

Carly Cat is licking the **envelope**.

eagle

The **eagle** has a sharp beak and sharp claws.

egg

The baby bird comes out of the **egg**.

escalator

Kelly Kangaroo rides down the **escalator**.

earth

The **earth** is round.

elephant

Ellie is an **elephant**.

abcdefghijklmnopqrstuvwxyz

escaping

Ff

falling

Sam Squirrel is **falling** off the tree.

The prisoner is **escaping** from jail.

factory

Derek Duck makes trucks in his **factory**.

family

This is Molly Monkey's **family**.

exercising

Molly is **exercising** on her exercise bike.

fairy

The **fairy** is flying.

farmer

The **farmer** grows corn on his farm.

21

abcde**f**ghijklmnopqrstuvwxyz

father
Leo Lion is the **father** of the cubs.

field
The sheep are grazing in the **field**.

fish
The **fish** is blowing bubbles in his bowl.

feather
Roger Rabbit has a red **feather** in his cap.

filling
Hilda Hippo is **filling** the bath with water.

fishing
Willie Worm is **fishing**.

fence
Sam Squirrel is sitting on the **fence**.

fire engine
The **fire engine** races to the burning fire.

flag
Kelly is waving a **flag**.

abcde**f**ghijklmnopqrstuvwxyz

floating

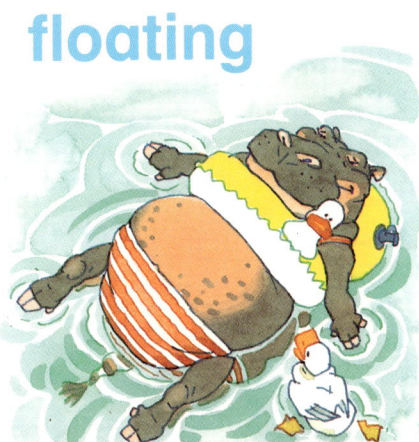

Hilda Hippo is **floating** on top of the water.

fork

Sometimes Boris Bear eats with a **fork**.

fox

The **fox** is stealing some eggs to eat.

flower

A big, pink **flower**.

fountain

Derek Duck is on top of the **fountain**.

frog

Freddie is a fat **frog**.

fly

The **fly** is climbing up the wall.

fruit

A big bowl of **fruit**.

23

abcdef**g**hijklmnopqrstuvwxyz

Gg

garden

Patsy Pig has a very pretty **garden**.

giant

A jolly **giant**.

game

Willie and Millie are playing a **game**.

gate

Freddie Frog leaps over the red **gate**.

garage

Derek Duck drives his car into the **garage**.

ghost

Derek Duck is dressed up as a **ghost**.

giraffe

Gertie is a **giraffe**.

abcdef**g**hijklmnopqrstuvwxyz

girl
Sophie is a **girl**.

glove
Roger Rabbit is wearing a baseball **glove**.

goose
The **goose** is chasing Derek Duck.

glass
A **glass** of lemonade.

goat
The **goat** is chewing Patsy Pig's apron.

gorilla
The **gorilla** beats his chest.

glasses
Willie Worm wears his **glasses** to read.

gold
A chest full of **gold**.

grape
Bill Bird is picking a **grape** to eat.

abcdefghijklmnopqrstuvwxyz

grapefruit
The **grapefruit** is on Boris Bear's plate.

ground
Willie Worm lives under the **ground**.

Hh

grass
Leo Lion is hiding in the tall **grass**.

guitar
Molly sings while she plays her **guitar**.

hamburger
A big, juicy **hamburger**.

grasshopper
The **grasshopper** hops over the grass.

gun
This is Roger Rabbit's toy **gun**.

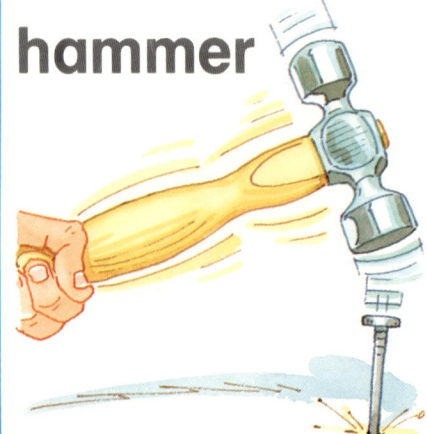

hammer
The **hammer** knocks the nail into the wood.

26

abcdefg**h**ijklmnopqrstuvwxyz

hamster
The **hamster** is Millie Mouse's friend.

hat
Gertie Giraffe is wearing her best **hat** today.

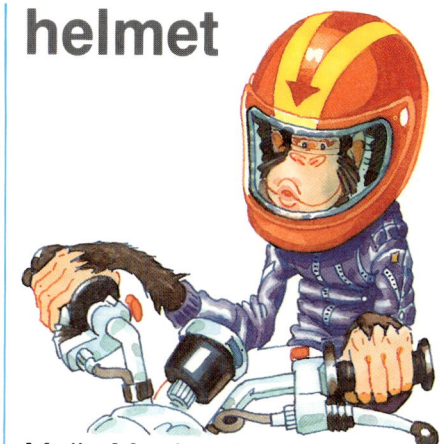

helmet
Molly Monkey has a **helmet** on her head.

hanging
Molly Monkey is **hanging** by her tail.

hedge
Millie Mouse scampers along the **hedge**.

helping
Millie is **helping** Patsy to hang up the washing.

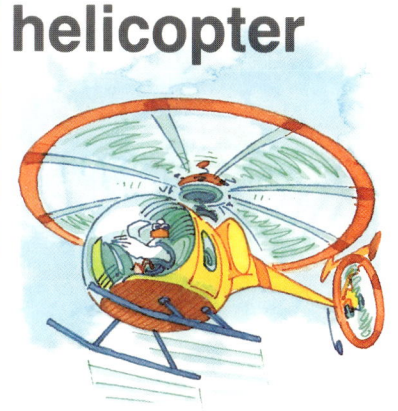

helicopter
The **helicopter** flies high in the sky.

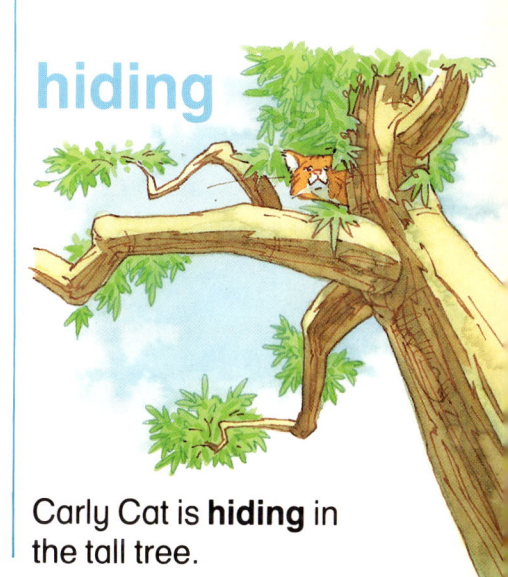

hiding
Carly Cat is **hiding** in the tall tree.

27

abcdefg**h**ijklmnopqrstuvwxyz

hill
Dudley Dog is running up the steep **hill**.

holiday
Patsy Pig goes on **holiday** every summer.

horse
The **horse** gallops off with Roger Rabbit.

hippopotamus
Hilda is a happy **hippopotamus**.

honey
A pot of runny **honey**.

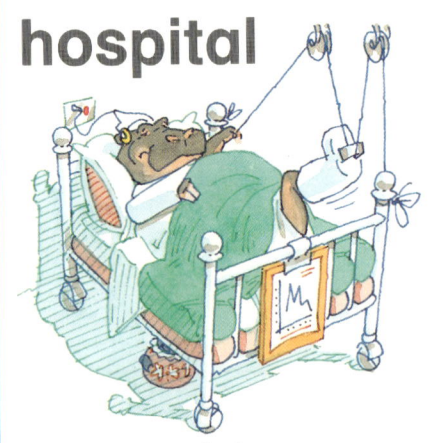

hospital
Hilda Hippo is in **hospital**.

hole
Sam Squirrel peeps out of the **hole**.

hook
The keys are hanging on the **hook**.

house
This is Millie Mouse's little **house**.

abcdefgh i j klmnopqrstuvwxyz

Ii

i

ice
Freddie Frog has fallen through the **ice**.

ice cream
Kelly Kangaroo loves to eat **ice cream**.

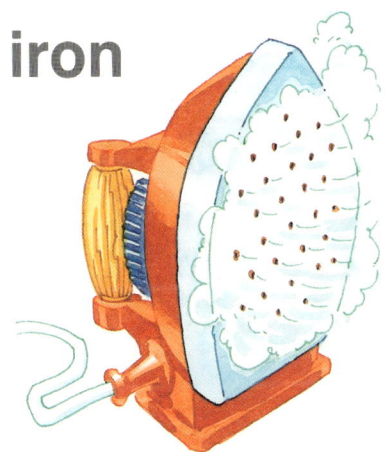

insect
A scary **insect** with a big sting.

iron
The **iron** is hot.

island
Bill Bird is all alone on the **island**.

Jj

j

jacket
Boris Bear has a new, striped **jacket**.

jar
There is one sweet left in the **jar**.

29

abcdefghi j k lmnopqrstuvwxyz

jeans
Boris Bear's **jeans** are hanging up to dry.

jug
A **jug** of orange juice.

Kk

jeep
The **jeep** drives over a bumpy road.

jumping
Freddie Frog is **jumping** over the hurdle.

kangaroo

jewels
Patsy Pig wears lots of sparkling **jewels**.

jungle
Lots of animals live in the **jungle**.

Kelly is a **kangaroo**.

abcdefghij**k**lmnopqrstuvwxyz

kettle
The **kettle** is boiling.

king
The **king** is sitting on his throne.

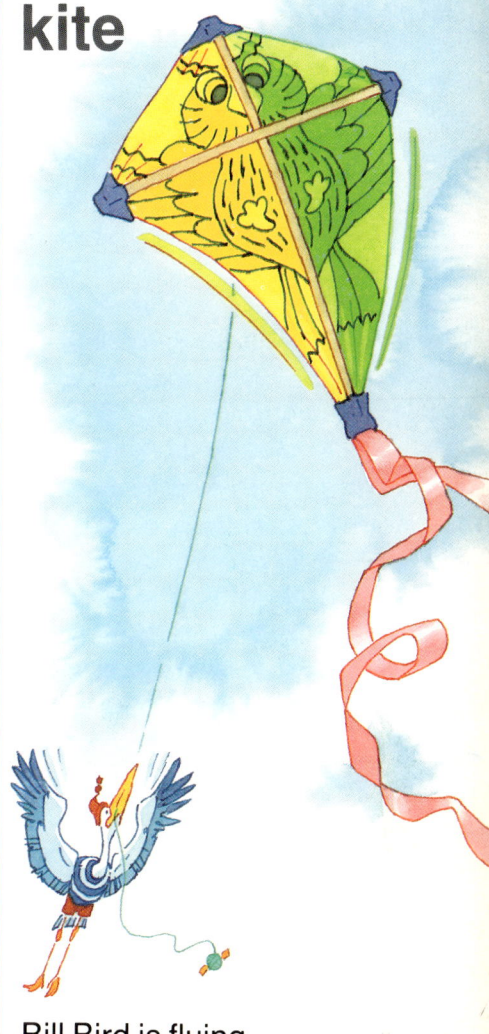

kite
Bill Bird is flying his **kite**.

key
Molly Monkey puts the **key** into the keyhole.

kissing
Millie is **kissing** Willie.

kicking
Roger Rabbit is **kicking** the ball.

kitchen
Patsy Pig is working in her **kitchen**.

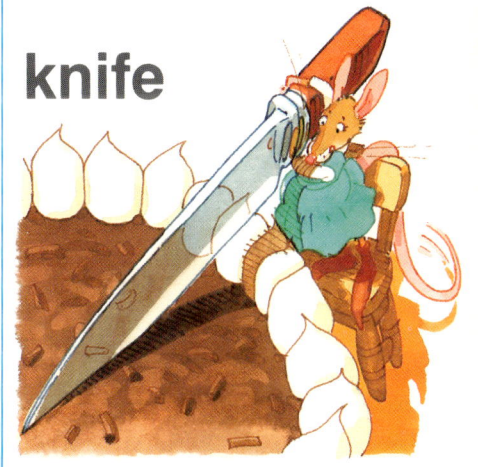

knife
Millie Mouse cuts the cake with a sharp **knife**.

abcdefghijk**l**mnopqrstuvwxyz

Ll

lamb

The **lamb** is chasing a yellow butterfly.

leaf

Freddie Frog is hiding under a green **leaf**.

ladder

Molly Monkey is climbing up the **ladder**.

lamp

Willie Worm has a **lamp** beside his bed.

lemon

The yellow wasp is on the yellow **lemon**.

laughing

Roger Rabbit is **laughing** at Derek Duck.

letter

Patsy Pig is writing a **letter** to Boris.

abcdefghijk**lm**nopqrstuvwxyz

lettuce

The caterpillar is nibbling the **lettuce**.

lion

Leo is a handsome **lion**.

Mm

m

lighthouse

Bill Bird is looking out of the **lighthouse**.

lizard

The **lizard** has caught a fly with his tongue.

lollipop

Millie Mouse is licking a red **lollipop**.

magician

The **magician** is doing a clever trick.

man

The **man** is wearing a blue, striped suit.

abcdefghijklmnopqrstuvwxyz

map

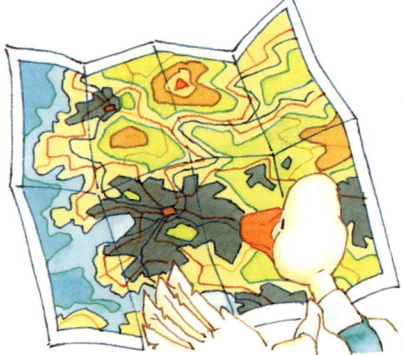

Derek Duck is looking at a **map**.

matches

Millie is naughty, she is playing with **matches**.

milk

Carly Cat has spilt the **milk** on the floor.

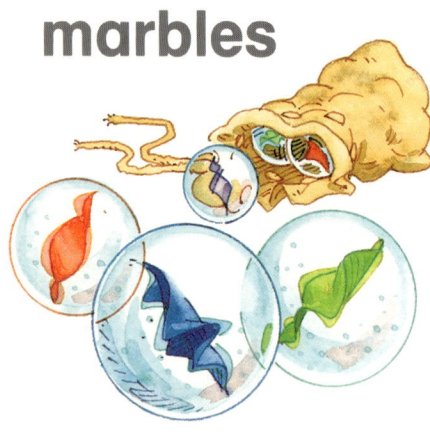

marbles

The glass **marbles** are different colours.

meat

The butcher has all kinds of **meat** in his shop.

mirror

Patsy Pig is looking at herself in the **mirror**.

mask

The **mask** makes Roger look like a monster.

medicine

The baby is going to have her **medicine**.

model

This is Derek Duck's **model** aeroplane.

abcdefghijkl**m**nopqrstuvwxyz

money
Boris Bear has lots of **money** in his hand.

mother
Molly is the **mother** of two little monkeys.

mouse
Millie is a **mouse**.

monkey
Molly is a **monkey**.

mountain
Bill Bird is on top of the high **mountain**.

mug
Boris Bear's **mug** is hanging on the hook.

moon
The **moon** is shining in the dark sky.

mushroom
Freddie Frog is slipping off the **mushroom**.

abcdefghijklm**n**opqrstuvwxyz

Nn

needle
Millie Mouse is threading the **needle**.

newspaper
Boris Bear is reading his **newspaper**.

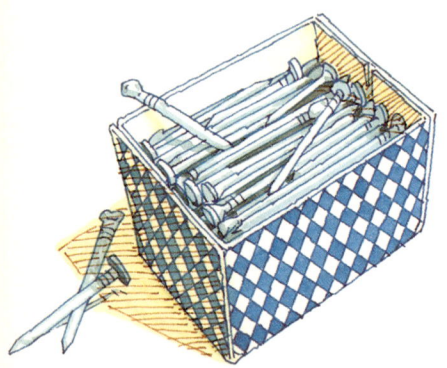

nails
There are lots of **nails** in the box.

nest
The two baby birds are in the **nest**.

nurse
The **nurse** is taking Hilda Hippo's pulse.

necklace
Patsy Pig's **necklace** is around her neck.

net
Willie Worm has caught a fish in his **net**.

nuts
Sam Squirrel has a big pile of **nuts**.

abcdefghijklmn**o**pqrstuvwxyz

Oo

onion

The **onion** is making Millie Mouse cry.

ostrich

octopus

Ollie is an **octopus**.

opening

Patsy Pig is **opening** a can of beans.

The **ostrich** is much bigger than Bill Bird.

office

Willie Worm works hard in his **office**.

orange

Molly Monkey wants to eat the ripe **orange**.

owl

The **owl** is sitting on a branch.

37

abcdefghijklmno**p**qrstuvwxyz

Pp

panda
The **panda** is eating a bamboo shoot.

park
Patsy Pig is meeting Boris Bear in the **park**.

painting
Millie is **painting** a picture of Roger.

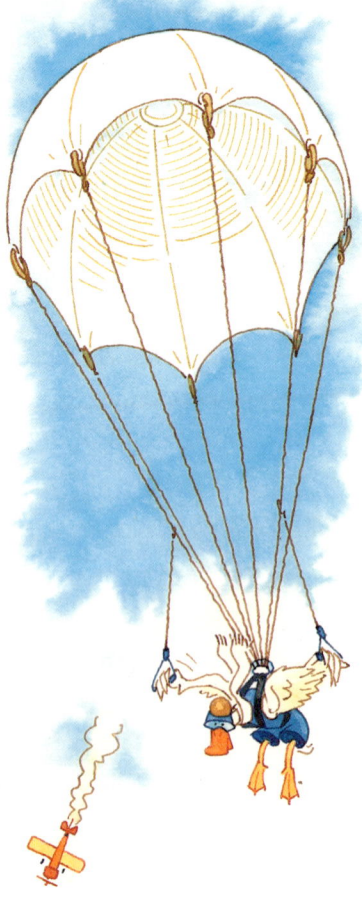

parachute
Derek Duck is coming down by **parachute**.

parrot
The **parrot** is swinging on his perch.

pancake
Patsy Pig is tossing a huge **pancake**.

party
The animals are having a wonderful **party**.

abcdefghijklmno**p**qrstuvwxyz

paying
Patsy Pig is **paying** Derek Duck for the food.

peas
Peas in a pod.

photograph
A bad **photograph** of big Boris Bear.

peach
A **peach** on a plate.

pencil
Millie Mouse is drawing with a **pencil**.

piano
Ollie Octopus is good at playing the **piano**.

pears
Pears on a pear tree.

penguin
The **penguin** is keeping her chick warm.

picking
Ellie Elephant is **picking** apples off the tree.

abcdefghijklmno**p**qrstuvwxyz

picnic
Willie and Millie are having a **picnic**.

pigeon
This is Derek Duck's pet **pigeon**.

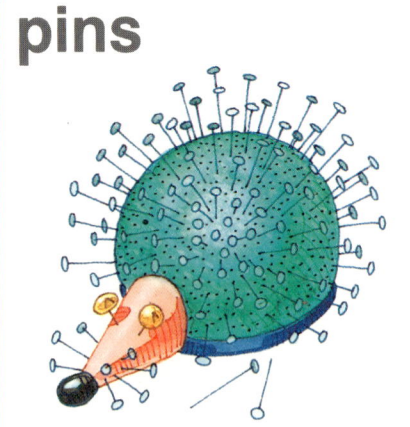

pins
The **pins** are stuck in the pincushion.

pie
A piping hot **pie**.

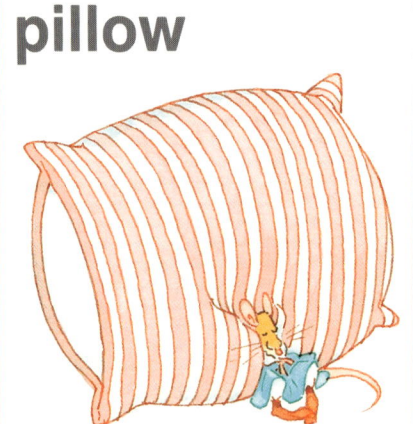

pillow
Millie Mouse is resting against a soft **pillow**.

pirate
Bill Bird, the **pirate**, is looking for land.

pig
Patsy is a pretty **pig**.

pineapple
Millie Mouse is tasting the **pineapple**.

40

abcdefghijklmno**p**qrstuvwxyz

pizza
A delicious, hot, cheese and tomato **pizza**.

playing
Freddie Frog is **playing** leapfrog with his friend.

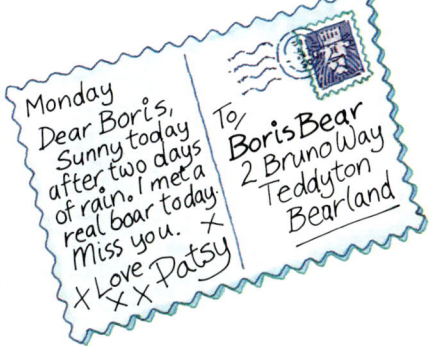

postcard
Patsy Pig has sent a **postcard** to Boris Bear.

planting
Patsy Pig is **planting** rows of poppy seeds.

pocket
Millie Mouse is peeping out of the **pocket**.

potatoes
A sack of **potatoes**.

plate
This is Boris Bear's best **plate**.

poppy
Patsy Pig has grown a beautiful, red **poppy**.

present
Ollie Octopus is opening his **present**.

41

abcdefghijklmno p q rstuvwxyz

princess
The **princess** loves the handsome prince.

puppet
Molly Monkey is playing with her **puppet**.

Qq
q

pulling
The cub is **pulling** Leo Lion's tail.

puppy
The **puppy** is chewing Boris Bear's slipper.

quarter
A **quarter** of the pie has been eaten.

pushing
Patsy Pig is **pushing** her piglets in the pram.

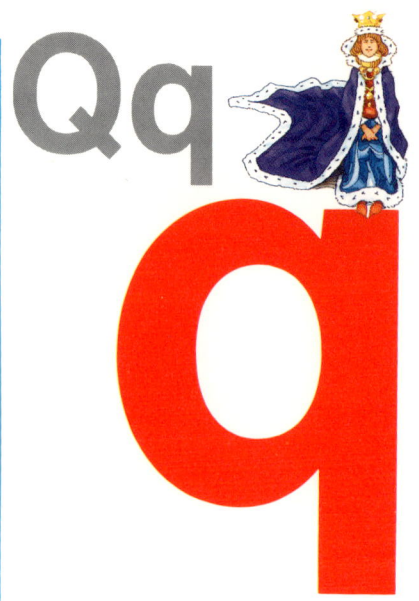

queen
The **queen** has a long purple robe.

abcdefghijklmnopq**r**stuvwxyz

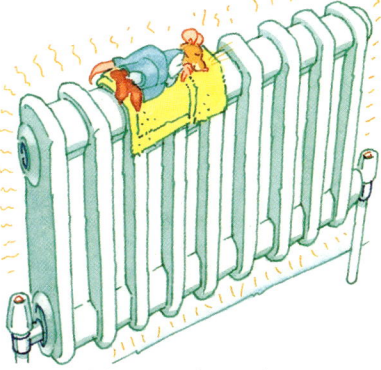

Rr

radiator
Millie Mouse is asleep on the warm **radiator**.

raining
It is **raining** hard.

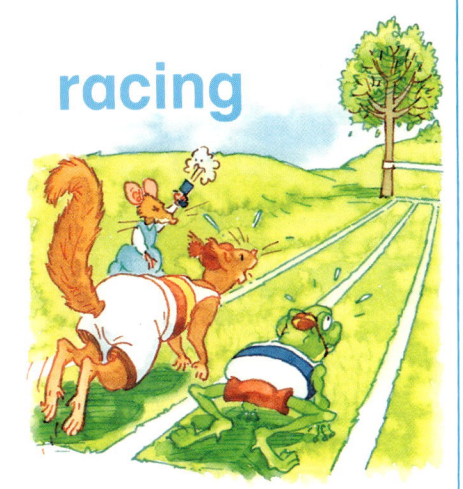

rabbit
Roger is a noisy **rabbit**.

radio
Dudley Dog is listening to the **radio**.

racing
Freddie Frog is **racing** against Sam Squirrel.

rainbow
There are seven colours in the **rainbow**.

rat
Millie Mouse is hiding from the **rat**.

43

abcdefghijklmnopqrstuvwxyz

reading
Willie Worm is **reading** in bed.

ribbons
Gertie Giraffe has lots of **ribbons** in her hair.

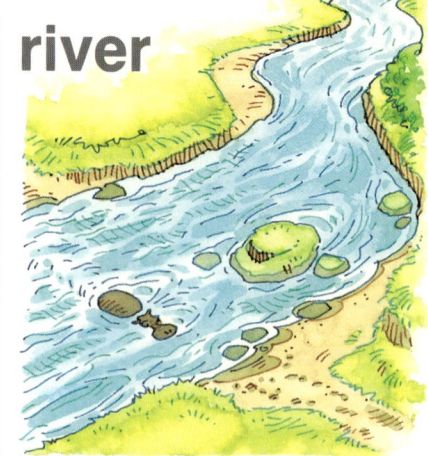

river
Hilda Hippo is swimming across the **river**.

record
Patsy Pig is playing her favourite **record**.

riding
The cub is **riding** on Leo Lion's back.

road
Derek Duck is driving along the winding **road**.

reindeer
Santa's **reindeer** has a red nose.

ring
Patsy Pig is wearing a **ring** on her finger.

robot
The **robot** can walk and talk.

44

abcdefghijklmnopq**r**stuvwxyz

rock
Freddie Frog is climbing on to the **rock**.

rocking horse
Millie Mouse is sitting on a **rocking horse**.

rope
Molly Monkey is swinging on a long **rope**.

rocket
The **rocket** blasts off to the moon.

rolling
The snowball is **rolling** away from Dudley Dog.

roof
Sam Squirrel is running up the steep **roof**.

rose
Patsy Pig is smelling the red **rose**.

45

abcdefghijklmnopqrstuvwxyz

rowing

Freddie Frog is **rowing** as fast as he can.

Ss

sandals

A pair of red **sandals**.

ruler

Molly is measuring her tail with a **ruler**.

sailor

Ollie Octopus is a **sailor**.

sandwich

A tomato, ham and lettuce **sandwich** for Boris.

running

Roger Rabbit is **running** as fast as he can.

sand

Hilda Hippo is buried in the **sand**.

sausages

Dudley Dog has stolen the **sausages**.

abcdefghijklmnopqr**s**tuvwxyz

saw
A sharp, shiny **saw**.

school
Willie Worm goes to **school** to learn.

seal
The **seal** is sunbathing on a rock.

scarecrow
The **scarecrow** doesn't scare Bill Bird.

scissors
Molly Monkey cuts the paper with **scissors**.

sewing
Patsy Pig is **sewing** on a button for Boris.

sea
Ollie Octopus is swimming in the blue **sea**.

shadow
Gertie Giraffe looks at her **shadow**.

47

abcdefghijklmnopqr**s**tuvwxyz

sheep
The **sheep** has two lambs.

shirt
Boris Bear's striped **shirt** is on a hanger.

shorts
Roger Rabbit is wearing his red **shorts**.

shell
Willie Worm has found a **shell** on the beach.

shoe
Millie Mouse is asleep in Boris Bear's **shoe**.

shouting
Molly Monkey is **shouting** at Derek Duck.

ship
The **ship** is sailing across the blue sea.

shopping
Kelly Kangaroo has been **shopping** today.

shower
Hilda Hippo is having a nice hot **shower**.

abcdefghijklmnopqr**s**tuvwxyz

signpost

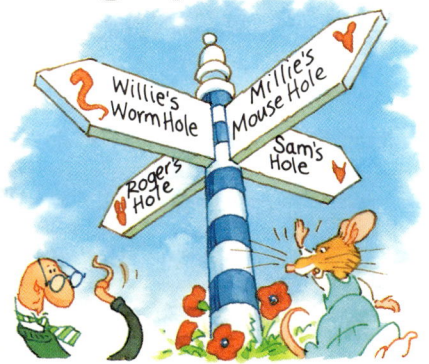

The **signpost** shows Millie the way to go home.

skeleton

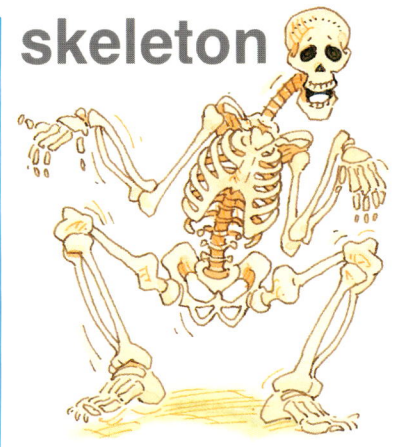

A smiling **skeleton**.

slide

The animals are sliding down the **slide**.

sink

Freddie Frog is swimming in the **sink**.

skiing

Derek Duck is **skiing**.

skates

These are Molly Monkey's new roller **skates**.

sleeping

Boris Bear is **sleeping** very soundly.

slippers

Freddie Frog jumps into Boris Bear's **slippers**.

49

abcdefghijklmnopqr**s**tuvwxyz

smelling

Boris Bear is **smelling** the apple pie.

snow

Sam Squirrel is covered with **snow**.

soap

The pink **soap** is in the soap dish.

snail

The **snail** is making a slippery trail.

snowman

Millie Mouse is looking up at the **snowman**.

socks

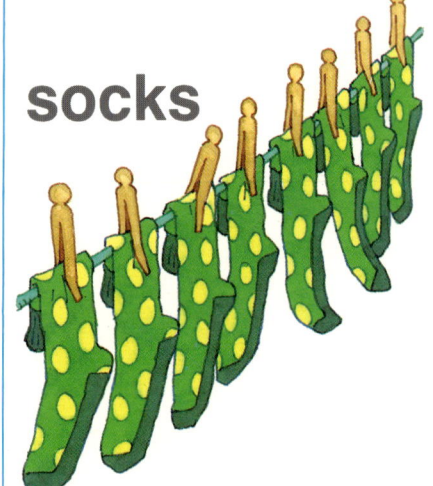

Ollie Octopus's **socks** are hanging up to dry.

snake

A slithery **snake**.

soldier

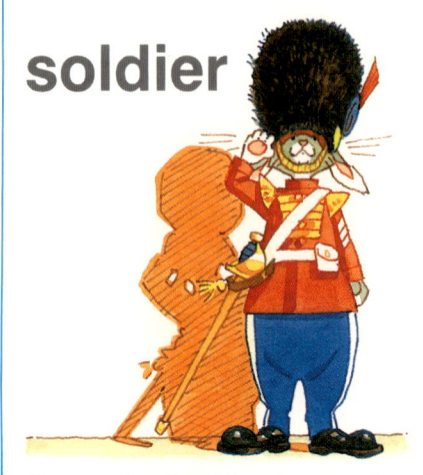

Roger Rabbit is dressed up as a **soldier**.

abcdefghijklmnopqr**s**tuvwxyz

spade

Willie Worm is sleeping beside the **spade**.

splashing

Freddie Frog is **splashing** Derek Duck.

stairs

Willie and Millie are climbing up the **stairs**.

spider

A scary, hairy **spider**.

spoon

Molly Monkey is feeding her baby with a **spoon**.

squirrel

Sam is a hungry **squirrel**.

stamp

There is a picture of Leo Lion on the **stamp**.

51

abcdefghijklmnopqr**s**tuvwxyz

star

The **star** shines brightly in the sky at night.

stool

Millie Mouse is sitting on a green **stool**.

string

Carly Cat is unwinding the ball of **string**.

station

Patsy Pig is waiting at the **station** for a train.

straw

Molly Monkey drinks through a striped **straw**.

submarine

The **submarine** is deep under the sea.

stealing

The thief is **stealing** some jewels.

strawberries

A plate of delicious, red **strawberries**.

sun

The hot **sun** shines down on the yellow sand.

abcdefghijklmnopqr**st**uvwxyz

sunglasses

Patsy wears **sunglasses** in the hot sunshine.

swan

The **swan** carries her baby on her back.

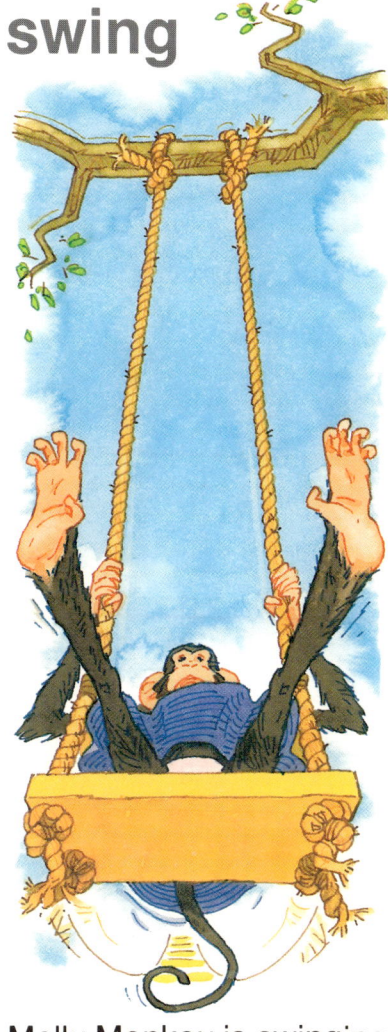

swimming

Freddie is **swimming** as fast as he can.

swing

Molly Monkey is swinging on the **swing**.

sword

Roger Rabbit is playing with his toy **sword**.

Tt

table

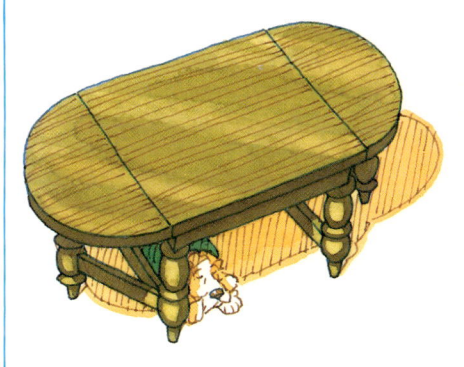

Dudley Dog is lying under the **table**.

tadpoles

The jar is full of tiny **tadpoles**.

53

abcdefghijklmnopqrs t uvwxyz

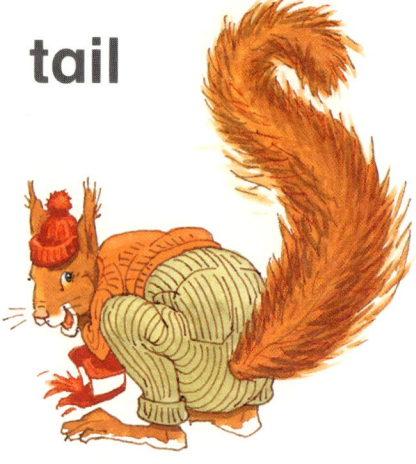

tail

Sam Squirrel has a long, bushy **tail**.

teddy bear

The **teddy bear** is blue and white.

television

Carly Cat is watching **television**.

taxi

Gertie Giraffe is riding in the **taxi**.

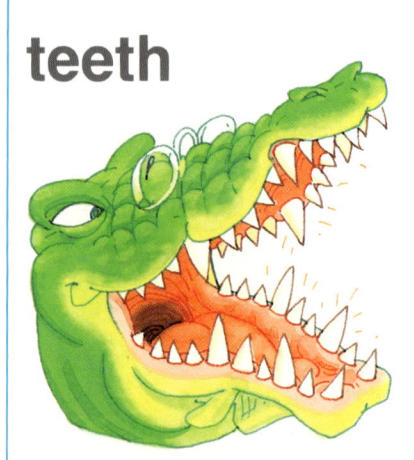

teeth

Old Croc has lots of sharp **teeth**.

tent

Dudley Dog is fast asleep in his green **tent**.

teacher

The **teacher** is writing on the board.

telephone

Patsy Pig is talking on the **telephone**.

thief

The **thief** is climbing out of the window.

abcdefghijklmnopqrs**t**uvwxyz

thimble

Patsy Pig has a **thimble** on her finger.

tie

Willie Worm is wearing a green and white **tie**.

toothbrush

Old Croc's **toothbrush** has lots of bristles.

throwing

tiger

The **tiger** is roaring.

toothpaste

Millie Mouse squeezes the tube of **toothpaste**.

Roger Rabbit is **throwing** the ball into the air.

tomato

A juicy, red **tomato**.

towel

Hilda Hippo dries herself with a huge **towel**.

abcdefghijklmnopqrs**t**uvwxyz

toys

There are lots of **toys** on the floor.

train

The **train** speeds down the railway track.

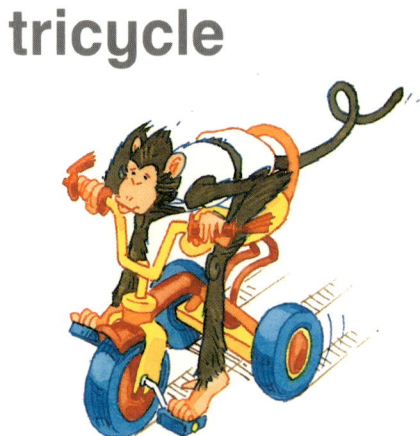

tricycle

The baby monkey is riding a **tricycle**.

tractor

Derek Duck is driving a **tractor**.

tree

trousers

Boris Bear has a patch on his **trousers**.

traffic lights

The **traffic lights** have changed to green.

Bill Bird is hiding behind the fir **tree**.

truck

The **truck** is dumping the dirt.

56

abcdefghijkrs**t**uvwxyz

trumpet
Ollie Octopus is blowing his **trumpet**.

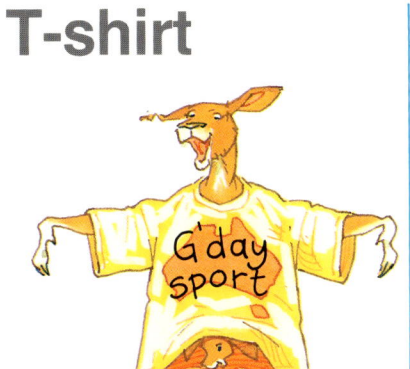

T-shirt
Kelly Kangaroo is wearing a big **T-shirt**.

turkey
A gobbling **turkey**.

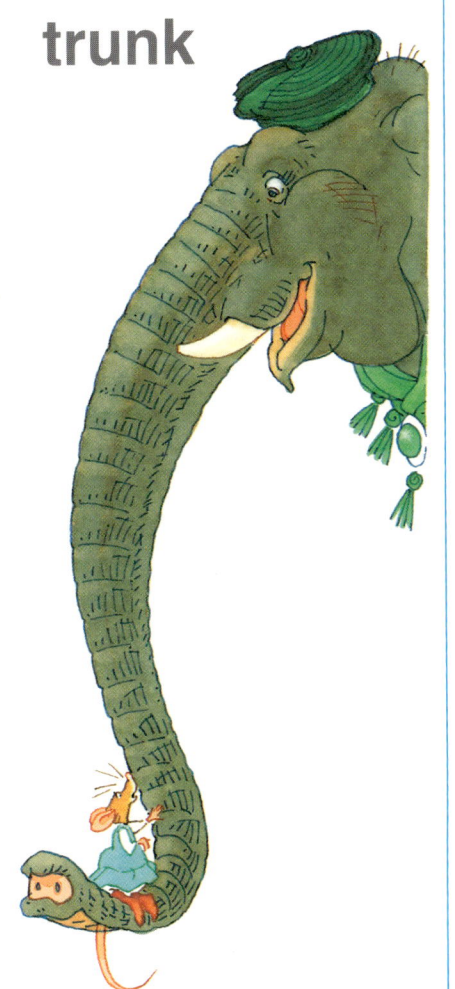

trunk
Millie Mouse sits on Ellie Elephant's **trunk**.

tulips
Two **tulips** in a vase.

twins
These girls are **twins**.

tunnel
The train is going through a dark **tunnel**.

typewriter
Willie Worm is typing on his **typewriter**.

abcdefghijklmnopqrstuvwxyz

Uu

Vv

u

v

violin

Molly Monkey is playing the **violin** softly.

umbrella

The big **umbrella** keeps Derek Duck dry.

vacuum cleaner

Patsy cleans the carpet with a **vacuum cleaner**.

volcano

undressing

Molly Monkey is **undressing**.

vegetables

Willie Worm is hiding in a pile of **vegetables**.

Hot rocks and lava burst out of the **volcano**.

58

abcdefghijklmnopqrstuvwxyz

Ww

W

washing

Molly Monkey is **washing** her baby.

watch

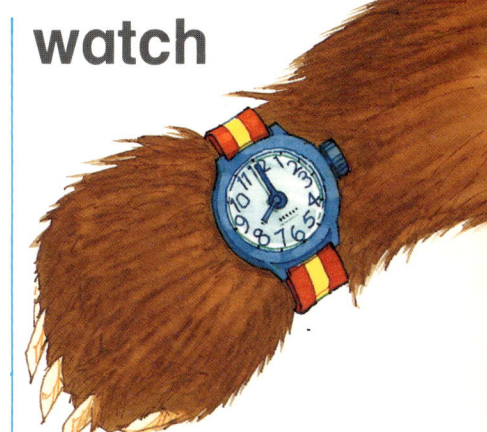

Boris Bear is wearing a **watch** on his wrist.

walking

Leo Lion is out **walking** with his cubs.

washing machine

Willie Worm's tie is in the **washing machine**.

whale

The **whale** gives Ollie Octopus a ride on his back.

wall

Sam Squirrel is running along the brick **wall**.

wasp

The **wasp** has stung Roger Rabbit.

59

abcdefghijklmnopqrstuv**w**xyz

wheel

Derek Duck has taken the **wheel** off his car.

windmill

Bill Bird lands on top of the **windmill**.

witch

The **witch** flies around on her broomstick.

whiskers

Leo Lion has beautiful, long **whiskers**.

wood

Sam Squirrel sits on the pile of **wood**.

whistle

Roger Rabbit is blowing his **whistle** loudly.

window

Carly Cat looks out of the **window**.

writing

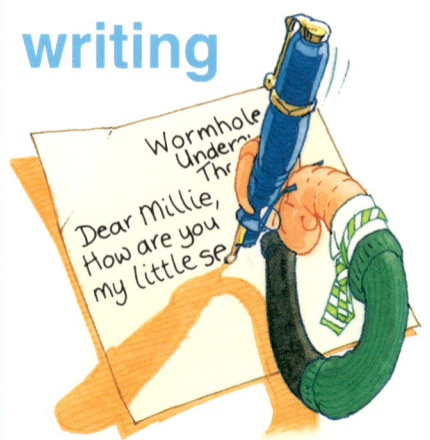

Willie Worm is **writing** a letter to Millie Mouse.

abcdefghijklmnopqrstuvw**xyz**

Xx Yy Zz

x y z

x-ray

Hilda Hippo holds up an **x-ray** of herself.

yacht

Derek Duck is sailing his **yacht**.

zebra

The **zebra** has black and white stripes.

xylophone

Ollie Octopus is playing the **xylophone**.

yawning

Leo Lion is **yawning**.

zoo

The Word Gang are at the **zoo**.

61

Extra Words

Parts of the body

- bottom
- hair
- head
- ear
- shoulder
- back
- eye
- nose
- cheek
- mouth
- lip
- neck
- tongue
- chin
- knee
- tummy
- elbow
- finger
- hand
- arm
- leg
- foot
- toe

Colours

- red
- orange
- yellow
- brown
- green
- blue
- pink
- purple
- white
- black

62

Numbers

1 one
2 two
3 three
4 four
5 five
6 six
7 seven
8 eight
9 nine
10 ten

Shapes

square
circle
oval
triangle
rectangle
star

63

Designer: Edward Kinsey

First published in 1988
Reprinted 1989
Conran Octopus Limited
37 Shelton Street
Covent Garden
London WC2H 9HN

© 1988 Conran Octopus Limited

All rights reserved.
No part of this publication may be
reproduced in any form or
by any means without prior
permission in writing of the publisher.

ISBN 1 85029 145 4

Printed in Hong Kong